LET'S READ

AV²

BY WEIGL™

ADDED VALUE • AUDIO VISUAL

Go to **www.av2books.com**, and enter this book's unique code.

BOOK CODE

V358955

AV² by Weigl brings you media enhanced books that support active learning.

AV² provides enriched content that supplements and complements this book. Weigl's AV² books strive to create inspired learning and engage young minds in a total learning experience.

Your AV² Media Enhanced books come alive with...

Audio
Listen to sections of the book read aloud.

Key Words
Study vocabulary, and complete a matching word activity.

Video
Watch informative video clips.

Quizzes
Test your knowledge.

Embedded Weblinks
Gain additional information for research.

Slide Show
View images and captions, and prepare a presentation.

Try This!
Complete activities and hands-on experiments.

... and much, much more!

Published by AV² by Weigl
350 5th Avenue, 59th Floor New York, NY   10118
Websites: www.av2books.com   www.weigl.com

Library of Congress Cataloging-in-Publication Data
Carr, Aaron.
 Jefferson Memorial / Aaron Carr.
      pages cm. -- (American icons)
 ISBN 978-1-4896-2898-5 (hardcover : alk. paper) -- ISBN 978-1-4896-2899-2 (softcover : alk. paper) -- ISBN 978-1-4896-2900-5 (single-user ebk.) -- ISBN 978-1-4896-2901-2 (multi-user ebk.)
 1. Thomas Jefferson Memorial (Washington, D.C.)--Juvenile literature. 2. Jefferson, Thomas, 1743-1826--Monuments--Washington (D.C.)--Juvenile literature. I. Title.
 F203.4.J4C37 2014
 975.3--dc23
                                    2014038567

Printed in the United States of America in North Mankato, Minnesota
1 2 3 4 5 6 7 8 9 0 18 17 16 15 14

112014
WEP311214

Project Coordinator: Heather Kissock
Designer: Mandy Christiansen

Every reasonable effort has been made to trace ownership and to obtain permission to reprint copyright material. The publishers would be pleased to have any errors or omissions brought to their attention so that they may be corrected in subsequent printings.

Weigl acknowledges Getty Images, iStock, and Alamy as the primary image suppliers for this title.

CONTENTS

2   AV² Book Code

4   What Is the
    Jefferson Memorial?

6   A National Symbol

8   Planning the Memorial

10 Building the Memorial

12 The Right Stones

14 Grand Opening

16 Finishing the Statue

18 In the Memorial

20 The Jefferson Memorial Today

22 Jefferson Memorial Facts

24 Key Words/Log on to
    www.av2books.com

What Is the Jefferson Memorial?

The Jefferson Memorial is a building in Washington, D.C. It has a large statue of Thomas Jefferson inside.

A National Symbol

The Jefferson Memorial was made to honor Thomas Jefferson. He helped the United States become a country. He later became president of the United States.

Planning the Memorial

People began to plan the Jefferson Memorial in 1934. It was to look like a well known building in Rome.

Building the Memorial

Work began on the memorial in 1938. President Franklin D. Roosevelt laid the first stone in 1939.

The Right Stones

Most of the Jefferson Memorial is made from a kind of stone called marble. This marble came from four different states.

13

14

Grand Opening

The memorial was finished in 1943. An event was held to open the memorial. The event marked 200 years since Thomas Jefferson was born.

Finishing the Statue

The statue was made from plaster at first. This was later changed to bronze.

In the Memorial

A dome covers the inside of the memorial. People can read the words of Thomas Jefferson on the walls.

The Jefferson Memorial Today

More than two million people visit the Jefferson Memorial each year. People can visit the memorial at any time of day.

JEFFERSON MEMORIAL FACTS

These pages provide detailed information that expands on the interesting facts found in the book. These pages are intended to be used by adults to help young readers round out their knowledge of each national symbol featured in the *American Icons* series.

Pages 4–5

What Is the Jefferson Memorial? The Jefferson Memorial is one of the most iconic structures in the Washington National Mall. The memorial is located on 18 acres (7 hectares) of land along the Potomac River Tidal Basin. It is about 1 mile (1.6 kilometers) south of the White House. The memorial is 129 feet (39 meters) tall.

Pages 6–7

A National Symbol Thomas Jefferson was one of the most important figures in early American history. As a Founding Father, Jefferson worked to free the American colonies from British rule. He is best-known as the author of the Declaration of Independence. However, he was also first secretary of state, second vice president, and third president of the United States.

Pages 8–9

Planning the Memorial The Jefferson Memorial was announced in 1934 as part of a plan to make the nation's capital more beautiful. The memorial was designed by architects John Russell Pope, Otto R. Eggers, and Daniel P. Higgins. Although the design was largely based on the Pantheon in Rome, it also drew inspiration from the rotunda at the University of Virginia. The rotunda was designed by Jefferson.

Pages 10–11

Building the Memorial Some people did not like the plans for the memorial. They felt it should be more modern. Others did not like the chosen location. President Franklin Roosevelt approved the design and location to allow construction to begin. He then laid the cornerstone on November 15, 1939.

Pages 12–13

The Right Stones The stones used to make the memorial are symbolic. The outside of the memorial is made from Vermont marble, the inside walls are Georgia marble, and the floor is Tennessee marble. A marble ring around the statue is made of Missouri marble. The statue itself stands on a base of Minnesota granite. Indiana limestone makes up the inner ceiling. These stones symbolize the country's original 13 colonies and its expanded Union.

Pages 14–15

Grand Opening The Jefferson Memorial was opened with a dedication ceremony on April 13, 1943. This was the 200th anniversary of Thomas Jefferson's birth. President Franklin Roosevelt led the ceremony, which included about 5,000 people in attendance and millions more listening on the radio.

Pages 16–17

Finishing the Statue When the United States entered World War II in 1941, the use of metal was rationed. The original statue of Thomas Jefferson that sat in the center of the structure was made from plaster that had been painted bronze. Metal rationing ended after the war, and the statue was replaced with a 19-foot (5.8-m)-tall bronze statue in 1947. The statue was sculpted by Rudolph Evans.

Pages 18–19

In the Memorial The memorial can be entered through four columned entrances. Above the memorial's main entrance is a pediment that shows Jefferson reading the Declaration of Independence. The interior is a large, open space with a high, domed ceiling. The inside walls are inscribed with quotations from Jefferson.

Pages 20–21

The Jefferson Memorial Today According to the U.S. National Park Service, the Jefferson Memorial is the third most-visited presidential memorial in the country. It has an average of 2.3 million visitors each year. The memorial is open 24 hours a day. Park staff are present each day from 9:30 AM to 11:30 PM, and tours are offered every hour between 10 AM and 11 PM.

KEY WORDS

Research has shown that as much as 65 percent of all written material published in English is made up of 300 words. These 300 words cannot be taught using pictures or learned by sounding them out. They must be recognized by sight. This book contains 47 common sight words to help young readers improve their reading fluency and comprehension. This book also teaches young readers several important content words, such as nouns. These words are paired with pictures to aid in learning and improve understanding.

Page	Sight Words First Appearance
4	a, has, in, is, it, large, of, the, what
7	country, he, later, made, to, was
8	began, like, look, people, well
11	first, on, work
12	came, different, four, from, kind, most, right, states, this
15	an, open, years
16	at, changed
19	can, read, words
20	any, day, each, more, than, time, two

Page	Content Words First Appearance
4	building, Jefferson Memorial, statue, Thomas Jefferson, Washington, D.C.
7	president, symbol, United States
8	Rome
11	President Franklin D. Roosevelt, stone
12	marble
16	bronze, plaster
19	dome, walls